# I wi ep
# trying!

With thanks to Catherine Veitch and Elissambura.

Miles Kelly

Oma the orangutan wanted to be good at everything.

She loved trying new things, but she always wanted to be the best at them.

One day her friend challenged her to build the very best tree nest.

Oma began collecting the biggest, softest leaves.

But **WHOOSH!** suddenly a storm cloud burst overhead and rain flooded Oma's new nest.

"**GO AWAY!**" Oma shouted at the rain. "Look at my soggy bottom!"

My nest is ruined!

Oma was determined to create the best nest. So, she tried to build the next one super-fast.

She whipped off branches and made her nest as fast as she could...

...but the rain soon came back and drenched it all.

Oma didn't believe them.
"I can prove it," replied Vina.

When it stopped raining Vina gave
Oma and Amir a young seedling each.
"Plant these," she said.

Amir planted his seedling where it had shelter and light, and the rain dripped gently on to it.

Oma hid hers in the hollow
of a dry, dark tree.

After a week, Amir's sapling had five new
leaves but Oma's hadn't grown at all.

After two weeks Amir's sapling had grown tall and strong. "The rain has helped my tree to grow!" boasted Amir.

Oma's sapling looked wilted and brown. The sunlight and rain hadn't reached it at all. Oma felt sad.

I can see now, our forest needs the rain to grow.

"I'm not the best at building nests or growing trees," Oma sighed.

"But you're the best at trying your best!" laughed Amir. "Every time something went wrong, you kept trying," said Vina.

Can you think of a time when you had to keep trying your hardest?